DIVINELY INSPIRED

DIVINELY INSPIRED

TRAUMA TRIUMPHED

VOLUME 1

REGINA SCALES

J MERRILL

J Merrill Publishing, Inc.
434 Hillpine Drive
Columbus, OH 43207
www.JMerrill.pub

Library of Congress Control Number: 2024902278
ISBN-13: 978-1-961475-17-5 (Paperback)
ISBN-13: 978-1-961475-20-5 (Hardcover)
ISBN-13: 978-1-961475-18-2 (eBook)

Book Title: Divinely Inspired
Author: Regina Scales

CONTENTS

CONTENTS

BITTER MOTHERS, BROKEN LOVERS

Bitter mothers, broken lovers,
Undeveloped sons, rejected loved ones,
Abused daughters, wayward fathers —
Self-accountability has gone south,
Babies are taken out from cries to have food in
their mouths.

Inconsideration is the new inflation,
As food becomes scarce, and laborers cower in-
side in fear.
Fields of faith in apostate, replaced by machines
and trending things.
They do as they are told,
Without attitude to behold,
Nor do they hear or respond to the kicks,

When you're constantly stubbing your toe.

Looking up, it appears dim,
As hearts become bitter once again from lack of
love toward the Creator,
Though there is no love greater.
It calms every storm and chastens with a warning
before they even come.
It shelters from the rain of any kind of pain,
And causes life to carry on and shine, beyond un-
derstanding and perception of the natural eye.

The cycle of violence is fueled by hate,
And the more it grows, the further we get from
the gate.
Turn your hearts to love,
In spite of,
Unconditional is possible, though not often spo-
ken of.
Rid yourselves of the toxicity hidden in your
heart.
And replace it with God's Word; then the healing
can start.

Confront those fears and bad decisions, confess
them, and repent.

Jesus came to save us, and He's on his way back,
my friend.
I call you friend, as He does me,
'Cause now you know what He's doing.
He went to prepare a place and upon His return,
Those you killed outside His will,
The innocents sacrificed and slain, left in the dirt,
Will rise first.

When He asks you about that bitter root that you
allowed to grow out of you,
Be prepared to walk away because then it's too
late,
You refused to let love undo the broken in you,
And you sowed it into others,
And now that blood is required of you—the bitter
mothers and broken lovers.

THE CONFRONTATION

What you won't do is cause me to go back.
I walk in abundance. No longer do I lack.
I live in abundant faith.
I get it. That grief came to distract,
But you seem to have forgotten I'm a warrior,
The most powerful of my many hats.
God created me to come through victoriously,
In spite of what you throw.

I won't ever give up!
Defeat is not in me. This you already know.
I can't lose 'cause my God has never lost.
Even when I wasn't worthy and sho' 'nuff dirty,
He counted up and paid the cost.

My life is in Him, and I understand you've been here,
But know this: His perfect Love will cause me to persevere in the face of any type of fear.

When you come in like a flood, by the power in His Blood,
I will overcome.
When I look up, my strength will be renewed,
As He raises the standard against you.
And I can resist you, and you have to flee,
'Cause that's how submission to Him has empowered me.

At the sound of His name, every knee, even thee, has to bow.
So, who's the big guy now?
Thank you for pressing me,
You let me know He considers me worthy,
Or else you wouldn't be allowed to trouble me so much.
I recognized the familiarity of your touch.

I am His anointed, called, and equipped.
Yeah, I know you thought you gained some ground when I threw that little fit.
His Word says I can be angry; just do not sin.

His joy is my strength, and within me, He ever
lives to make intercession for me.
He'll go before me to keep me and remain to the
very end.

So, see ya' later, hater,
His glory for me is what waits.
That destruction you set as a snare for me will
trip you up on the way to that lake.
Of fire, that is, 'cause that's all you're gonna get,
'Cause your destiny is already set.
God and I are the majority,
And He's not done with me yet!

DECEPTION AND THE HOLY SPIRIT

They flatter with their lips and appearance, but God is not in it.
They entice with the device of deceit that sounds so sweet,
But will leave a bitter taste that forces you to run without haste to the fountain of deliverance,
'Cause you've allowed an intruder to enter through the filter of your ear,
And he's set up shop in your heart to devour the power of God's Word hidden within,
To liberate you from sin, by causing you to doubt and keep your head to the ground,
Hoping you fall and not look up at all, to the hills from whence comes your help.

This deceiver is all about self.
They love your company when failing miserably
to stand on their own.
They seek whom they may devour as they aim-
lessly roam,
To and fro, setting traps of despair, long and
flowing like hair,
To get you entangled and entrapped,
And brush you over with lack of joy as they toy
with your emotions.
And try to choke out your purpose and dreams
with the disturbance of what appears to be defeat.

But greater is He that is within,
So, you must tap in, through humility, when the
enemy has you down in the valley.
God is the Lily there, and you are never too far
for Him to hear your prayer of repentance.
He is willing to forgive and able to restore the
hope you lost when you didn't count up the cost,
Of whether their words were genuine or
profound.
When you became attracted to the distorted
sound and tainted message of their intent,
Which was to draw you in just to drop you off the
cliff of discontentment,

and send you spiraling down from the hope you
have found,
That caused you to stand and undo the plan of
destruction.

By touching Heaven through your faith and trust
in God,
'Cause He is the Way, the Truth, and the Life.
And now you see this thief who showed up in
your night season of your life for who he really is
—a robber of destiny.
Commit your ways unto the Lord, and you can
resist.
He'll make your enemies your footstool as He
prepares the table before them.
Perfect love for Him will dispel all fear,
And you'll be strengthened again to overcome
being misled from walking by sight,
and see through your spiritual eye afar off, long
before he ever gets close,
The way of escape provided, and revealed
through the Holy Ghost.

HIM

She wasn't impressed with His style of dress; she was captivated with His scent. He would often go away, but it would linger until He returned again. It signified the essence of His presence, though tangible it was not. It created an image she could hold on to, for He was the center of her thoughts. She wrapped herself in the savor of the sweetest memories that would arise. She was wide open and attentive to receive what He would feed into her spirit, the things she beheld with her eyes.

In her heart, she felt His spark that ignited the fire of His love. She had tried many times outside of, but His fit like a glove. It covered, protected, and comforted like no other. At times of discipline, it felt fatherly, but it was always supportive, like a big brother. It was everything she desired, so she never retired in her pursuit. His love was never changing and powerful to change the old to All things new.

It was new every morning; like the dew, it would just sit. Its beauty was paralyzing, something you could never forget. She would bask in it for hours and become empowered to overflow. That left a smile, so it was all worthwhile. It illuminated her from within, so outwardly she would glow and grow further in Him, like a blooming flower, increasing over time on the vine. In Him, she would abide and produce fruit that would never sour. She would ripen to perfection with His reflection consistent upon her, oozing at the seams, as He manifested her dreams and desires while elevating her higher and higher.

Her every delight was in Him, the conqueror of her heart. He was most exclusive, so that made the choosing of another something she didn't need to bother. She left the choices up to Him, even when it came to whether to connect to the proposition of a friend. See, if they were anything opposite of Him, the connection would have to be broken because, according to the word He spoke, it was apparent they would be unequally yoked. Their character was not in agreement with His, nor did it resemble. Often, she would tremble, but only in fear of the decision to ignore Him and the outcome of disobedience. But her perfect love for Him cast out that fear because, from Him, it wasn't given.

So, she gained victory when she got free from wondering. Obedience to Him was better than the sacrifice of their rejection that was sure to come later when He revealed the greater in her that He alone would do, upon her willingness and availability to be used by Him when He spoke of the disappointment in their choices made for selfish gain. He was her judge, so she would not budge from His will. She would stand in the power of His might and endure the battle He would fight. She would endure to receive the crown of His glory, adorned with precious jewels that represented the souls she would win for Him as she walked in her deliverance. He brought her out of doubt, and she stepped in faith onto the path He ordered for righteousness' sake to follow His lead into her destiny, which He foreordained when He chose her to bear His name. She is now the image of His light for the world to see, a representative, set apart and holy, saved by grace through faith, submitted only to Him. The Lover of her soul is who she came to know.

I LOVE YOU MOST OF ALL

I love you most of all.
Your love is my song.
My song of you keeps me singing all day long.
My heart cries for you to abide and never leave.
Then I remember your promises to me.

Faithful through the ages you've been,
More than a brother, sticking closer than a
friend.
Your spirit surrounds me in times of fear.
The more you speak, the more I wanna hear.

I love to get lost in time, captivated by this song
of mine.

Still and resting in your presence, in your peace, I
hide.
Tears overwhelm my face in our secret place, and
you catch every one.
Hope in you keeps me together so I don't become
undone.

My strength is renewed as I wait in you,
And I can dance in the glory of this divine tune,
That nothing compares to.
A melody sweet enough to move me in the most
compassionate of ways,
Strong enough to keep every enemy at bay.

A rhythm and a flow of its own,
Never changing yet mesmerizing, tangible
enough to hold.
Its words empower me to shine.
Oh, how I love to delight in this song of mine.

It's transformed and renewed in my mind,
Washed away the old and redeemed my life.
It helps me to fight every battle and come
through victoriously.
It's ever-present and ever-living, making inter-
cession for me when I'm weak.

Jesus, you are love, and this is the song that I'll keep singing my whole life long.

LET ME TELL YOU ABOUT MY FRIEND

L et me tell you about my friend! We get up and spend time with one another every morning as if we've never been in each other's presence. It's always so calm and serene in moments like these. He helps me to see the most beautiful things. He doesn't spare me the correction or redirection from the things he sees as displeasing within me. He lovingly corrects and never disrespects or rejects—at least up to this point. He promised not to, and his word has never faltered. It's a joy to my ears, and my heart smiles from the love I feel within, coming from him.

He's got this crazy way of bringing to my remembrance the stuff and things I need to see and how they relate to the decisions I make that are or could possibly devastate. As he shows me a different way of moving, it's so soothing to my mind that I become engulfed, and there's nothing more I want than to give him all of me. Because in his presence, I'm so free to be and become. To someone else, it may sound dumb that I'm so caught up. But when times get rough, I just focus on us, which always brings me back to the place of peace I've found in the moments spent with the most amazing friend I've ever known.

He called me friend first and then adopted me when he promised to never leave, even said he would be with me and go to the very end. He defeats all my enemies through the power of his word that he teaches me. Now, ain't that some foolishness? He does stuff like that to throw the know-it-alls off when they think themselves higher than us. He teaches me to pour from an empty cup as he fills me with His eternal love. I'm renewed and humbled. This is the one relationship I cannot and will not fumble!

It is possible to become distracted, and at times I was. But he just sat back and waited till I got done hating in and on me for what others had not appreciated while I debated with him about the quality and royalty he called me when he chose me and molded me through the calamity that had befallen me. He's suffered and endured way more than I've gone through, so I turned back with godly sorrow and let him love me from that new beginning. I want to be more like him, so every chance I get, I delight myself in him because he always was and is. And he also said that when my suffering ends, I can reign with him in his kingdom. Amazing!

No other friend has come close or can even compare. I'm so glad I finally embraced this, so now I handle our time with care. Because when the evil of this world tries to take me there, his spirit will make me aware of movement, revealed in times of sitting still, as he manifests in silence the strategy of success for me and the schemes of my enemy along with the way of escape for me to gain victory. My God, how I needed a friend like this! I would have no hope if it weren't for him. See, he laid down his life for all mankind and rose again. That power in his word, yeah, that's all in his name. My friend's name is Jesus, and he's available to you too. He told me to share him with you because he wants time with you as well, to give of himself. He's got plenty more; he stored it up so we could spread him around. When you need him, call him; he will show up.

Honor and respect his presence, and he will keep you afloat. With him before you, nothing can harm you. Trust him; this guy is no joke. He's the way, the truth, and the life. His light brightens the darkest of days, and all his ways lead to victory. Don't take my word for it; again, call him, and you'll see. He'll stick closer than a brother when you submit and let him love you from your soul, where your will and emotions grow. And who knows, you may grow to love him like I do, or even more. And that's cool, too, because as I brag and boast about him, I'm really just exposing you to his truth. I've done my part and shared. Now, the rest is up to you!

PROPHESY

Prayer is not a message being sent for us to do nothing with. It has come as an answer for direction and protection from a force outside and beyond our understanding, leading us to a place of peace as He gains the victory once again over death and destruction. He's guiding us to glory if we would but reflect on how he freed the slaves from bondage. Miracle after miracle, he's still performing. He's the same God that moved back then. Right here and now, we have an opportunity to turn from our wicked ways and bow to the One, True, Sovereign King and follow His lead.

We must walk this out daily, trust and not doubt. Don't look back, complain, or do the former things with the new wine or the skin of deliverance when He brings us into this new place. Some days may seem harder than others, but use them to encourage your brothers that as long as we keep going, without even knowing, our faith is growing every day, for without it, it is impossible to please Him who is leading. By day and by night, he has us covered and hidden in Him. He's right in it with us and will see us through to the end.

So today, we'll celebrate Him, who we believe in for deliverance and protection from all spiritual and physical inner enemies. Within us dwelleth no good thing except the Creator dwells therein. It's because of Him we stand a chance. So do not fear! Don't be afraid; freely lift your hands or do your dance. Every enemy is defeated. He's doing it again so we will understand that He chose us to use us in His plan of redeeming lost man. Worship Him only! There is none greater. Die out to selfish desires and live, love, support, and build one another. Become one body unified in love with the power from on high working on our behalf, covering us in the blood of the covenant that sealed the deal from generation for generations to come. He's healing the land and our hearts. This is our brand-new start. This is the day of victory for the days we pray to see.

The territory flowing with milk and honey (the resources) and the giants (challenges) are nothing impossible for the King of Kings (the Greater in Thee) or the power and authority in His name, in which we are given along with dominion. With Him before us, nothing can stand before Him, and at the sound of His name, when they bow to Him in us, we must remain humble as He changes and transforms minds from what once was. We will be used to undo the course that would befall and restore the lost. Adhere to the call and be set apart. Do not conform to familiarity, and He will begin to manifest redemption, which was always His plan from the beginning. Believe for it, reach for it, and pursue it. We are empowered to possess it. Rest in it. There is no deception in Him. His word will be accomplished, and He is faithful who sent it. For all the promises of God in Him are Yes, and in Him Amen, unto the glory of God by us.

REFLECTION

It began with the way the sun reflected on the building. It was so beautiful and unique that I began to think of the Son's reflection on me. The light He has shined on my life radiates from the inside out. Of this, I have no doubt. I'm always in awe of His beauty and the way it moves me, that even when I'm down, its comfort reflects a smile. I'm reminded of all the tears I shed through the years that no longer form as the result of the storm, but they stream down from the glory of the joy that has been restored. Yesterdays are just a memory away and only remind me of the time He kept me when I was lost. They've become treasures of endless measure, stored in heavenly places and unable to be consumed by moths. I can access them when I need to pull from their wisdom to sow a seed of compassion and understanding that will heal the continuous bleeding and remove the stain of guilt and shame experienced by my siblings, who bear the same name.

You see, I am my brother's keeper as a reflection of He who has kept my mind in perfect peace from the chaos and manipulation that once controlled me and drove me like a vehicle into the ditches of despair, hoping I would die there. I'm reminded of how He found me, beaten with the bruises of life, hidden within myself, surviving in strife, working against and not in time, absent from reality, and spiritually blind. No longer on my own, the mercy and grace extended and shown have awakened me to my rightful place, healed from a broken state. The ashes of my past and fragments of my pain reformed into bountiful baskets left to sustain. Impacted with provision from the precision of the divine, the Author and Finisher of my faith has illuminated His way to life and that more abundantly as a reminder of the promise to never leave or forsake me. He is the greatest love I've ever known, and my mind is blown every time I remember how gentle, loving, and kind is this Rewarder I sought to find.

STRAIGHT TALK

I couldn't be afraid to walk away from the pain that was killing me inside when trying to hide behind open eyes to the deceit and manipulation that was using me and confusing consistently with those unstable ways that counteracted the words they would say. I had to get out from the cloud of doubt that reigned over me to see that freedom from disbelief was calling to and waiting on me in those late-night hours that tried to devour my hope. I could no longer cope with the discontent within that was causing me to blend in and accept the sin of being less than who God created me to be.

I am His chosen gift, given to man to help him understand He is the Way, the Truth, and the Life, and because He is not a man that He should lie, who was I to live it? So, the decision I had to split it and choose better than the letter so I could live in, for, and with Him, by offering up prayers of repentance.

I had put my trust in man and my dependence on Him into hands and hearts that only worked deceit, and they had begun to consume me. But God saw my oppression, and I had learned enough of the lesson, so He provided a way of escape to bring me back to the path He had laid. He comforted my heart when I said goodbye with tears in my eyes to all that I had known and the dreams that were shattered and blown by empowering me to shake the dust from my feet upon realizing I had not been received. I had been tolerated to ease the loneliness and the desire of an unexposed source through a familiarity of sorts that sought to curse and destroy the blessing of the Lord.

I am the pearl that was cast before swine to be trampled under feet. Once torn into pieces, but now restored to reveal His glory once more. I am no longer the forgotten or forsaken; I am the adopted of the Faithful. I am the child of God who overcame the hardness of trials while in denial, now enlightened to stand alone and apart. I have yielded my heart to the Lover of my soul, and He is taking me to all the places I never imagined I could go.

SORROW

I saw you crying that day, but I admit, I stood off to see if the praise that was exclaimed when they mentioned your name was what I would see. Because I'm honest in saying it was your grief that drew me. I heard something in your tears that screamed in my ears, a sound only to be heard by the undisturbed spirit; otherwise, I could not hear it. The pleas from your knees were ridden with pain, and I almost broke at the sight of that strained vein. I remembered your face, as distorted and distraught as it was. A certain glow had gone dim, and I prayed you would find it again. I prayed you would remember that day you laughed until you cried. I prayed for your strength to remain from what brought you so low and left you so broken

I declared you would stand in your inner man and live to be great another way because you were depleted at the core and could take nothing more. I spoke healing to your heart with restored confidence, and a fight kicked in like no other. You rose like bread slow and steady, wiped your eyes dry, and popped your neck and shoulders for the ready. It was on and popping, and you weren't the One who would be stopping! "That is your baby, Lord, and she is on the move. Let her feet be steady and swift, her tongue to speak only your wisdom, allow her to express the pain effectively with sternness and temperance, and provide a way of escape during moments of temptation. Let her heart be heard through every true and genuine word; let no mistake be made with the message you want displayed. Her strength is for your glory, and as you reveal her story, you will be revealed in the expression of how she feels."

I saw you crying that day, but I'm honest in saying I stood off praying to see the praise they exclaimed when they mentioned your name. "If you see your brother in need and shut up your bowels of compassion, how dwells the love of God in you?" The Bible says, "Be angry, and sin not." We all have days or moments of anger or despair. Returning evil for evil is sin. If we honor the time given to express our anger or grief toward the individual or the situation to God and allow Him to bear the weight of it because He has borne every grief and carried every sorrow, then He will come into that situation with His grace and teach you to display the peace that He has given and the strength He has restored, to empower you to express yourself in a way that will win your brother, even though they have done you wrong, and bring unity and understanding, which is the ultimate victory!

LOST BOYS

Lost boys are like broken toys; you can't find them and play with them the same way ever again. Once located, you have to figure out how to reconnect with the boy within the man, and playing has to be removed altogether from the plan. This boy will be all about work because he's hiding behind his masculinity from the rejection and pain in which he's suffering. He's crying real loud with the silence he gives out.

He's working his own plan while laying hands on the women who won't forgive him for beating them into submission to his hurt as he tries to arise and find a way out from under his self-inflicted curse. He knows he needs someone, and that's definitely what he wants, but he's lost in sense and reality while self-destructing with powerful frailty. He's damaged goods, but that's the part you don't see. His mind has wandered away from his dream of home; therefore, he continues to roam.

And then the Lord says, "I am here; do not fear. I know my image has been distorted, but my plan I won't abort it. I know it's hard to see, and you fear belief in me from what left you lying there without a care like you had no purpose. I know that's a strange word but this, boy, is no toy and you're gonna be glad you heard this! You were created to be a son, and though within you feel undone, I finished the work on Calvary, and now I invite you to come. Lay all your cares and burdens down; you're lost to them now, but in me, you are found. I'll resurrect what's died in you, forget the former being; I make all things new."

"I'll teach your hands to war for the kingdom, a fisher of other men you'll become and overcome by my blood when you stand in the power of my might, but you must surrender the warring in your members and let me fight the battle. I have the strategy for you to succeed; I just need you to follow willingly and learn of me. My ways are not your ways, and this is how I restore."

"You feel that flutter in your heart? That's me knocking at your door. Let me fill you with my light; it expels and exposes everything that's dark. Direction is in subjection and surrenderance to me; no need to wander aimlessly. Humble yourself and seek me because lost boys are not impossible, but you must believe for what you don't see. That's called Faith, and without it, you won't see or be able to please me. I'm no thief in the night; that's your enemy, and he will try to deceive. Fear not; I will never reject or abandon you, and as I was with Moses, with you, I will also be. I am the voice you heed to now; your guilt and shame are mine, and you, I have justified. Apply your armor and stand. In due time, I will exalt the lost boy, forgotten by the hands of man, and you'll be found whole in me, living and walking out my plan for your expected end."

AWAKENING THE DREAMER

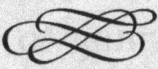

Oone day she refused to believe the lies and disbelief that she couldn't actually be someone great like the woman she kept seeing in her dreams. She was just a girl wandering sound in her own world, most of the time. She avoided being seen because when she was, she was almost never in love. Abuse, misuse, and blame could have been her name, at least that's what she adopted when no one stopped it to remind her she was a queen and she could do all things because that was the meaning of the name she was given, but the lesser she was living.

She had dope hope with genuine intent when she approached them and tried to connect on the level of a friend, but rejection is what she endured every time she wiped her tears from the floor of her pain, compounded by the stain of the shame she hid in her heart as a result of the things that went on in the dark. She rose every morning with a warning to not believe because belief was a delicacy only meant to be eaten by her oppressor because they saw themselves as better.

Oftentimes, she would speak her mind to their discontent with the wisdom that exceeded her age, so they numbered her days in strife and beat her into submission because she was too clever and never would she be better than those who stood above her, so with their refusal to love her she forgot to love herself.

Though she would keep going and growing, she could never mature past what they had implanted until Jesus found her later and began to recreate her from the circumstances of the hands of man. On the true potter's wheel, broken down, he began to rework his plan. He shaped her with strength from the weakness sent with the intent to destroy her, threw out the cup of hate that tried to seal her fate, and filled her up with love of a different kind, quite rare, understand, hidden from the natural eye.

Her rebirth was crafted by the master; in his image she would rise and shine before her enemies victorious. No longer inglorious, she would stand in her divine purpose, without repaying evil for evil but showing forgiveness and humility empowered by the king of kings, the queen he designed her to be. She would stand to rule nations in remote locations around the world with her worship for the author and finisher of her faith, the one they tried to block out in her younger days.

She would extend herself again without fear of acceptance, despite their non-believing perceptions, and declare her freedom from their bondage and pray for mercy for their souls to return so they themselves would not succumb to the destruction that had been brewing in their own hearts. She had been set apart to be silent with her yielded tears from past and present years to see his salvation while he undid the manipulation and devastation that kept her falling and down.

He would present her with a crown. Her prize for not letting go of her faith to endure as a good soldier and fight her way through with grace. Goodness and mercy would keep her enemies off her back as she kept her focus on the hills when they attempted to distract with rehearsed words in hopes to bring her again under the curse of non-production and poverty. She was blessed to live, exceeding and abundantly in the peace he promised to leave.

Beyond all understanding, it was her for him, from the beginning until he brings her to her expected end. Her deliverance is the evidence of her expectancy that someday his face she would see when she prayed, "let not mine enemies triumph over me." He would reveal his glory through the story of her life she would tell to all who listen and hear, in hopes that they too would believe for what life's circumstances would not show. When life deals you a boatload of grief and unbelief, you must search deep within and consult with the Greater Than, Father, Friend of the Holy Spirit within, and cover yourself with the thoughts he thinks according to his word concerning you. You are a chosen generation, a royal priesthood, a holy nation, a peculiar people, that you should show forth the praises of him who has called you out of darkness into his marvelous light. Greatness is in you and greater works will you do because he now lives in you. Receive beauty for the ashes that soiled you and stand in the power of his might. Give no thought to the former distorted vision of the broken girl but live in light of the overcomer who became the woman in the dream the girl kept seeing.

WAIT!!

I had to wait in abundant faith for the Lord to reveal the way and make my path straight. See, I had wandered off without counting the cost of being lost and outside because I chose not to abide out of pride and resentment toward the evil intent to separate me from what I deemed to be family. My kind was rejected because my heart reflected the light of right, though broken inside. I expressed myself without the help of those who would harm me because I allowed them to charm me with their evil deceit, so they betrayed me.

I couldn't see my way through nor figure out what to do, so I hung my head low and embraced what I didn't know. See, all I knew was pain, rejection, and the lack of acceptance. I looked like defeat, stained and shamed by sin. I was all alone with no one I could trust as a friend and had no hope of ever having one again until Jesus came. He showed up in His divine time and began to unwind the web of deceit that had encompassed me. He broke me down, repurposed my frown, and gave me a smile. He breathed into me the *Word* of life that undid the strife of trying to be like those who forced me to fight in the dark of night to keep my sanity in the daylight. He shined His light just right to illuminate the path to bring me back. Step by step, He ordered me and never left me, changed my mind, restored my spiritual sight, and gave me an ear to hear His voice ever so clearly. He didn't spare me the pain; he just reworked it for my gain, and then He changed my name.

No longer broken, He calls me Chosen. When I feel the familiarity of rejection, He reminds me I am accepted. No longer a part of the crowd, He called me out and set me aside for His use despite the abuse. It made me Greater, not a hater. It made me humble, so I no longer mumble through sounds of doubt. In confidence, I sing victoriously, and I cry aloud. I no longer cower in fear but stand in the Power of His might and rest with sweet sleep at night. I walk in alignment with Him even when the light appears dim. My total and complete trust is in Him, and I'm safer than I've ever been. Although I'm grateful to be a servant, He calls me Friend.

See what the enemy meant for evil? God has worked it for my good. What was once confusing is now clearly understood. No longer troubled on every side, He's given me peace and a secret place in Him I can hide, so when the evil and the wicked try to overtake me and present themselves again, He will already have revealed the strategy of success to defeat. I'll walk away with the win!

WEATHERIZATION

When the coldness of this world you pray to overcome, bask in Jesus, the Son. When man's bitter, frigid ways tempt you to hang your head low, oh, taste and see that the Lord is good, and He's the Lily of the Valley, you know! When hearts as cold as ice compel you to reconsider, comfort your soul in the warmth of His love and be not hindered. You are in this world, not of it, so wear its things as a loose garment, for they shall perish and wax cold, but you shall be changed and transformed. In the renewing of your mind, peace you shall find. The old familiar world won't even recognize you when all things are made new. You'll be seen in the image and likeness of the Creator, so you'll be persecuted for righteousness's sake because your promotion and elevation as a result of your humility will draw your haters.

Fear not, for the Lord is always with thee, and His Holy Spirit that lives within will alert and teach the ways of victory over every enemy. No weapon shall harm you, though it may form, and through the power in His name, you'll take dominion over every storm. You'll speak to the mountain by faith and tell it to be removed when you abide in Him, and His word dwells richly in you. Don't allow evil communication to disrupt your good manners but cover yourself in His divine blood and display it like a banner. Cry aloud and spare not. Cast down vain imaginations and bring into captivity every rebellious thought. Cast your cares on Him and get rid of any iniquity hidden in your heart. His Spirit cannot dwell in an unclean vessel, but He is willing and able, and you are nothing impossible. So, when the coldness of this world drops, let the fire of His word burn, making you a force that can't be stopped!

PRICELESS PEARL

Hey, young gurl, don't you realize you're a pearl, the rarest of kinds, quite hard to find, not crafted by the hands of man but formed from a grain of sand? In darkness, surrounded by hardness, you were crafted. A beautiful wonder to behold. Untouched and unharmed by the outside forces by divine design, you were brought forth. Small and unique, your splendor miraculous, cherished by the one who would find you, something unexplainable, a workman could not undo. You must be careful and aware of the hands you're in. They'll welcome you with pleasure, never recognizing the value you represent. They'll cast you to the side in their desire to devour. It is you who must recognize your power. You are fearfully and wonderfully made, a treasure of undeniable measure. With or without another, you possess the ability to stand alone. Though soft, your toughness is good, which is why your fragility is misunderstood. Your iridescence is illuminating. Oh, how you shine. You'll never decrease in value when cared for properly down through time. Your worth is priceless and set very high. Your genuineness is not to be compared cause another just like you you'll never find. Believe and receive the beauty that you possess. Never settle for or even accept less. If it does not match the quality or standard you amount to, don't try to make it fit. Have faith that what is meant to compliment is exactly what you are gonna get! Present yourself a living sacrifice, and the master crafter won't think twice about rewarding you with his truest desire.

Sincerely, your single submitted sister,
Regina F. Scales
Daughter of the King of Kings

ABOUT THE AUTHOR

Regina Scales, an author profoundly moved by her faith and life's intricacies, presents her literary debut, "Divinely Inspired." A beacon of devotion, Regina's journey is a testament to her unwavering faith in Jesus Christ and her dedication to a life of service and worship. As a proud mother to three natural-born and two cherished bonus children, Regina's family life is a rich tapestry of love and guidance.

Serving under the esteemed leadership of Apostle Larry A. Davis and Pastor Beverly Davis at the Fellowship Worship and Empowerment Center in Columbus, Ohio, Regina's spiritual journey is deeply rooted in community and leadership. Her professional life as a full-time cook and shift manager at a healthcare facility mirrors her commitment to nurturing and leadership, traits that spill over into her writing and personal endeavors.

Regina's passions extend beyond her professional and spiritual life into writing, where she channels her insights and experiences into words that inspire and empower. "Divinely Inspired" is a reflection of her journey, offering readers a window into the soul of a woman who finds beauty and strength in the everyday.

An avid lover of the outdoors, singing, and reading, Regina's interests are as diverse as her roles in life. Above all, she treasures her role as Gigi to her six grandchildren, whom she considers her greatest gifts. Regina Scales' biography is not just a narrative of her achievements but a celebration of a life lived with purpose, passion, and a deep connection to the divine.

facebook.com/regina.scales.52